SEVEN PRINCES *Of The* ANGELS

PRAYERS *WITH ANTIQVE Images*

Antonio del Duca

Translated by
Carmen de Pinopar

Seven Princes of the Angels Prayers with Antique Images

Original Latin text by Antonio del Duca.
In Venice in 1543, in Rome in 1555 and after Duca's death, in Naples in 1594 and 1604.

Translation, forward and appendix by Carmen de Pinopar.
Cover concept by Richard Cortes. Ian Hoyle from Stirling Print Solutions, technical assistance with the cover. Doug Heatherly from Lighthouse24, pre-flight tests and technical guidance in the final stages of production.

Duca, Antonio del, 1491-1564
[Septum Principum Angelorum Orationes Cum Antiquis Imaginibus. English]
Seven princes of the angels prayers with antique images / by Antonio del Duca; translated by Carmen de Pinopar.

ISBN 978-0-9953196-6-0 (softcover).

Published by:
House of Pinopar

FOREWORD FROM THE TRANSLATOR

The Catechism of the Catholic Church states in Paragraph 330: *As purely spiritual creatures angels have intelligence and will: they are personal and immortal creatures, surpassing in perfection all visible creatures, as the splendor of their glory bears witness.*

Angels are spiritual persons, that is, each one is a unique individual with a real personality and they are as different from each other as a human is different from another human. They are created beings, that is, even if they are immortal they exist within time as we do and do not know with certainty the future unless God reveals it to them. At the beginning of time the Angels were the living witnesses of the creation of the Universe, *the morning stars of creation,* and thus they are a "bit" more that 13.8 billion years old. They have superior intellects and in their long existence they have accumulated an immense amount of experience and thus through observation alone they can make an educated, if not a certain, forecast of where we may be heading without trespassing on our free will, our mental privacy or seeing into the future. Only God knows our thoughts. We can communicate telepathically with the Angels but they cannot read our mind without our permission. Even so, Angels can read micro expressions and other changes in our body far better than a lie detector, and so can the demons. Angels and demons can perform only natural and preternatural acts but the Angels can perform supernatural acts with God's assistance.

Demons desire to be adored and crave to take souls from God. To a good Angel it is abhorrent to be adored or worshiped or placed above God. The good Angels purpose is to assist the soul to ascend to God therefore communication and communion with them is to be cultivated. The devotee should look at the Angel as a mirror of God's perfections that are to be imitated.

The Eastern Orthodox Church names the seven Archangels in this order: *Michael, Gabriel, Raphael, Uriel, Sealtiel, Jehudiel,* and *Barachiel.* Their names appear on icons and prayers and the Church encourages the faithful to seek their intercession.

An Angel can intercede with God on behalf of his devotees to grant a request or to protect them. For instance, an Angel can perceive in real time that someone with the intention to harm his devotee is already waiting in ambush or that the airplane he/she has intention to board has a failing mechanical part that will bring the plane down and the Angel may ask God's permission to warn or inspire his protégé to take a different path or change the flight.

The history of the Roman Catholic Church's censure of these seven names is conflicted. As per the Vatican's 2001 *Directory on Popular Piety and the Liturgy, Section 217: The practice of assigning names to the Holy Angels should be discouraged, except in the cases of Gabriel, Raphael and Michael whose names are contained in Holy Scripture.*

The censure of all Angels names, except for the triad already mentioned, began in the year 745 at the second synod of Rome with Pope Zachary presiding over the trial of Aldebert *in absentia.* He was a colorful, charismatic and eccentric preacher born in Gaul. Modern scholars think that the heretic probably was a sincere visionary and perhaps a schizophrenic. He was viewed as a threat to the authority of Rome because he was a dangerously popular wandering bishop that promoted apostolic poverty and he was a colorful miracle wonder-worker with a rapidly growing multitude of followers among the humble country folk.

There is an indisputable need to exert caution when invoking by name energy beings because there are many spirit deceivers. The names of the Seven Princes of the Angels, with the exception of Michael and Uriel, are not the eight names invoked by Aldebert the heretic. They are the same seven names invoked by the Eastern Orthodox Church. Many Catholic Saints and Doctors wrote volumes in defense of the sanctity of these other ancient Angels names to no avail because of Rome's judgment of 745.

Then, in 1460, Archangel St. Gabriel appeared in eight raptures to Blessed Amadeus of Portugal, a famous mystic of impeccable character, a man beyond reproach and of proven sound mind who could not be fooled by a deceiver nor be dismissed as a "lunatic" nor labeled heretic. St. Gabriel shone new light on the *Revelation of St. John the Divine* and provided more information. Archangel Gabriel also revealed the names of the Seven Apocalyptic Angels who St. Gabriel specifically asked to be honored.

I pause here for a moment to remind the reader that all holy Angels are God's messengers by nature but Gabriel is God's Ambassador by excellence and he is known for being in charge of delivering the most important messages. Gabriel did not deliver to Amadeus his own message, he delivered God's message. It is not in an Angel's nature to desire for anything except for the Presence of God. Thus Gabriel would only ask to honor the Seven Apocalyptic Princes by name if it was the will of God and it promoted God's mysterious plans.

Blessed Amadeus wrote down St. Gabriel's message in the *Apocalypse Nova,* the New Apocalypse. The prophetic manuscript was secreted by Rome but not before a few hand-copies were made. In 1471, Pope Sixtus IV called Amadeus to the Vatican as his personal confessor and counselor, for the Pope recognized that he was blessed with the light from the Holy Spirit. It is to be noted that in the centuries following Amadeus other Saints and mystics claimed to have been in contact with the same Angels. Many wonders have been attributed to the Seven Princes' intercession and they are said to be especially effective in exorcising demons from locations and ending epidemics. Blessings were promised to those that cultivate their devotion.

The devotion was taught by Blessed Amadeus's sister Saint Beatrix da Silva to my ancestress Queen Isabel of Castile and so it began to be practiced by my family. The Church tolerated the Spanish monarchy and the Imperial House of Habsburg to invoke the Princes in private but they were pressured not to promote their devotion in public.

In 1516, ancient frescoes representing the Angels were discovered under the crumbling plaster of the primitive church of the Seven Angels (also called church of Sant'Angelo Carmelitano), in Palermo, Italy. Once the walls were restored, the portrait of each one of the Princes appeared accompanied by his name, personal symbols and attributes. These names were the same revealed by St. Gabriel to Blessed Amadeus. The images were set on a triptych.

Inspired by those ancient images, by the *Apocalypse Nova* and by subsequent mystic visions, the local priest Antonio del Duca became the Seven Princes' paladin. The Angels asked for a temple to be built in Rome over the ruins of the Baths of Diocletian where many captive Christians died during the construction. Among them was the group known as the Seven Martyrs: Saturnino, Ciriaco, Largo, Smaragdo, Sisinnio, Trasone and Pope Marcello. In that location there remained standing seven original columns and Duca inscribed on those columns the Seven Angels names as a pledge to build the basilica. This was an almost impossible mission considering the rigid position of the Catholic Church regarding the seven names.

To promote this goal and gain supporters, Duca published *Septem Principibus Angelorum Orationes cum ántiquis Imagibus,* The Seven Princes of the Angels Prayers with Antique Images. He handed the copies as gifts to prelates and people in positions of influence. This small book was printed in Venice in 1543, in Rome in 1555 and after Duca's death, in Naples in 1594 and 1604. In those later editions extra illustrations were added by a wealthy patron that knew well Duca's work and shared his passionate devotion to the Seven that stand before the Throne of God. I integrated diverse elements from the four editions to create this first English version.

The temple in Rome was commissioned to Michelangelo. It was completed and consecrated to St. Mary of the Angels and the Martyrs in 1564 shortly after Duca's death. One hundred years later Cardinal Albitius, at the service of the Inquisition, ordered that the names of the

Seven Princes be erased from the Basilica's seven pillars and from all the icons. Duca's little book was never reprinted.

The portrait of the group of the Seven Princes appears only in the later editions and it was taken from the third panel of the triptych, which had already been immortalized by the famous Hieronymus Wierix. In 1535, Queen Isabella's grandson the Holy Roman Emperor Charles V of Austria invoked the Seven Princes and defeated Barbarossa (Red Beard), the legendary Admiral of the Turkish fleet, saving Europe from the Ottoman invasion. In gratitude he commissioned Wierix to engrave the image of the Seven Princes as seen in the church of Palermo to promote their devotion through the Empire. The church was destroyed during a war in the 19th century and all that remains from the spiritual message of the frescoes is Antonio Duca's little book of antique images and the Wierix engraving. These images have been digitally restored by House of Pinopar.

I dared to translate *The Seven Princes of the Angels Hymn* with the guidance of Lander Meesun. I could not replicate the exquisite Latin Sapphic meter. There was no point for me to translate the prayer to the Guardian Angel and the Antiphon *Ave Regina Caelorum* and instead I used well-known versions.

To complement Duca's booklet and to expand the understanding of the Seven Sovereign Spirits and the Septenary, I have also published, *The Seven Princes of the Angels, St. Michael, St. Gabriel, St. Raphael, St. Uriel, St. Sealtiel, St. Jehudiel and St. Barachiel, The Septenary A Devotion to be Practiced in Private,* and four booklets exalting the nature of St. Michael, St. Gabriel, St. Raphael and our faithful companion, our Guardian Angel.

Hundreds of years ago Antonio del Duca said to the readers, *Valete faeliciter.* And so I also say now*, Farewell happy*!

SEPTEM

PRINCIPVM ANGELORVM

ORATIONES

CVM ANTIQVIS Imaginibus

OPERA

Antonij Ducæ Presbyteri Cephaludensis olim editæ.

CVM LICENTIA SVPERIORVM.

Ex Officina Horatij Saluiani.

NEAPOLI, Apud Io. Iacobum Carlinum, & Antonium Pacem. Anno 1594.

Antiphon of the Holy Guardian Angel.

God will put his Angels in charge of you, to protect you wherever you go. They will hold you up with their hands to keep you from hurting your feet on the stones. Alleluia. Alleluia.

V. Their Angels always see. Alleluia.
R. The face of my Father who is in Heaven. Alleluia.

Let us pray. Prayer.

Angel of God, My guardian Dear, to whom God's love commits me here, ever this day, be at my side, to light and guard, to rule and guide. Amen.

AVE REGINA CÆLORVM
AVE DOMINA ANGELORVM

Antiphon of the Most Holy Virgin Mother of God
And Queen of the Angels.

Hail, O Queen of Heaven.
Hail, O Lady of Angels
Hail! thou root, hail! thou gate
From whom unto the world, a light has arisen:

Rejoice, O glorious Virgin,
Lovely beyond all others,
Farewell, most beautiful maiden,
And pray for us to Christ.

V. Allow me to praise thee, O sacred Virgin
R. Against thy enemies give me strength.

Let us pray. Prayer.

Grant unto us, O merciful God, a defense against our weakness, that we who remember the holy Mother of God, by the help of her intercession, we may rise from our iniquities. Through Christ, our Lord. Amen.

Vbi eras cum me laudarent simul astra matutina, et iubilarent omnes filij Dei? IOB·38

Antiphon of the Holy Angels

Angels, Archangels, Thrones and Dominations, Principalities and Powers, Heavenly Virtues, Cherubs and Seraphs, praise the Lord of Heaven. Alleluia.

V. In the sight of Angels I will sing to Thee, O God.
R. I will worship facing Thy holy temple and confess Thy name.

Let us pray. Prayer.

O God, who dost dispense the services of the Angels and men in wonderful order; mercifully grant, that those who ever minister before Thee in heaven, may defend our lives here on earth.
Through Christ, our Lord. Amen.

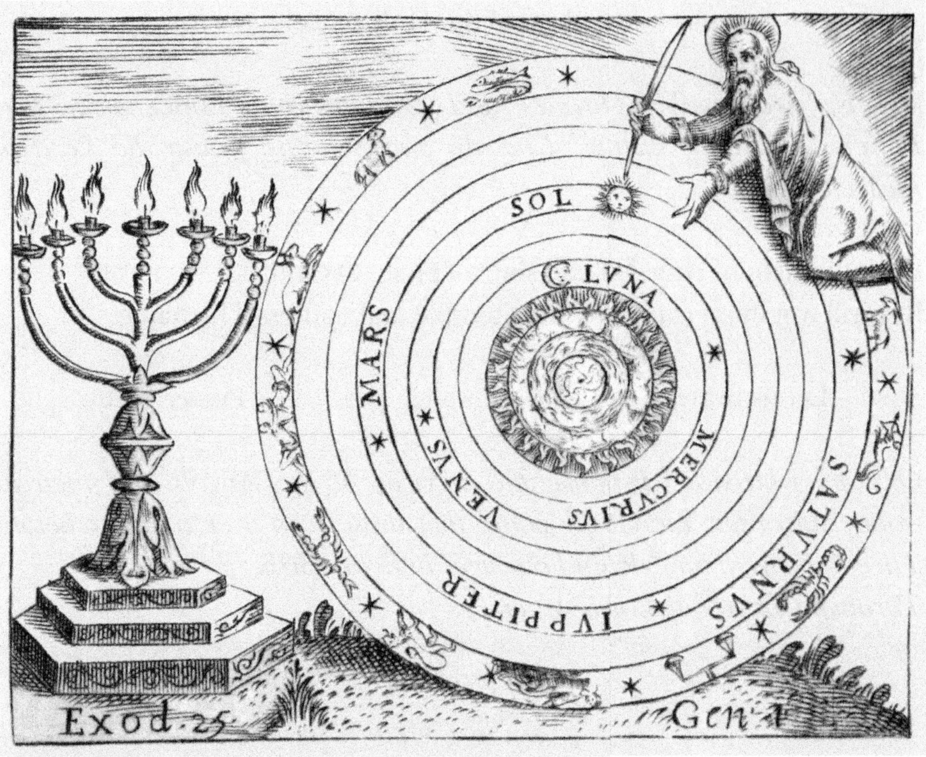

Antonio del Duca, rector of the Church of the Seven Princes in Palermo. In assistance of the pious reader of the Holy Angels.

O Most Christian Man: Of the Candlestick of seventy parts that on the order of God Moses made of pure gold, St. Jerome wrote that it signified the world with the seven wandering Stars [as it is interpreted by the historian] *Josephus, and by means of it St. Anselm admirably described a certain spiritual temple. We, however, assisted by Josephus and John the Evangelist, estimate that it represents the Church Triumphant with the Seven Spirits who are in the presence of God and in likewise manner, the existence of the Church Militant with the seven bishops who are dressed in bright Tyrian purple. It signifies as well the septiform temple that was built in Rome by the Holy Martyrs as from the vaticination of Isaiah: showing that we may also praise God in the marvelous temple of the Christians as wonderfully as the Jews did with the marvelous candlestick. Farewell happy!*

INTERPRETATION OF THE NAMES
OF THE SEVEN PRINCES OF THE ANGELS

MICHAEL	Who is like God?
GABRIEL	Strength of God.
RAPHAEL	Medicine of God.
URIEL	Fire of God.
SEALTIEL	Prayer of God.
JEHUDIEL	Confession or Praise of God.
BARACHIEL	Blessing of God.

Antiphon of the Seven Princes of the Angels.

O Seven Princes of the Celestial Militia who are in the presence of the Throne of God, to whom great tasks are entrusted for the protection of all the faithful, come to our aid, we pray, against the temptations of the demons and intercede for your devotees with the Immaculate Lamb, Son of God.

V. Adore the Lord. Alleluia.

R. The Princes of the Angels always stand in front of His Throne. Alleluia.

Let us pray. Prayer.

O God, who among all the other ornaments and gifts of Heaven, has ordained with marvelous method the ministry as well as the tasks of the blessed Angels for the government of the world: Grant us propitious, that through the seven Princes Assistants who always sit near You in a sublime throne, our life be protected. Through Christ, our Lord.

HYMN TO THE SEVEN PRINCES OF THE ANGELS

In Heaven the whole senate assembly was silent,
While the arrogant dragon engaged in war,
He who Michael trampled under his feet
And confined in the underworld.

We pay respect to you, Thundering Paranymph,
Whose Spirit resounds throughout the whole world,
Gabriel: fill our souls
With the light of Olympus.

O salutary Medicine of heaven,
Saint Raphael, bring the cure,
For the sick body and guide
The steps of the blind souls.

Uriel, Strong Ally of the good,
The power of the demons with the sword weakens,
Whose charity surpasses the vows
Of pious prayers.

Sealtiel, to you is in debt the whole world,
Whose Orator you are before the Father's Throne:
Supplicate that your servants' crimes
Are wiped clean.

May the dark duties of Judge Jehudiel,
Be far from us miserable ones, until,
The Grace of the Supreme Father
Washes out our crimes.

Our Helper, we implore that you favor,
Barachiel, everyone: remember us,
And refer the saints to God, we pray
With diligent action.

To the Triune God, Deity of the soul,
Praise, honor, virtue and likewise power,
Always decorum and blessings
For all eternity. Amen.

1. FIRST DAY: Antiphon of Saint Michael Victorious.

There was silence in Heaven, while the Dragon engaged in battle, and Michael fought him and obtained victory.

V. Prince Michael, come to the aid of your people.

R. And he remained to help the souls of the righteous.

Let us pray. Prayer.

O God who gave the glorious victory over the most arrogant Demoniarch to blessed Michael, the assistant Prince and supreme commander of the army combating under the banner of the Saving Cross that was provided for in eternity; we pray that by fortifying our forehead with the sign of the Savior, and by invoking the name of the aforementioned Triumphant Michael, you will grant us strength & victory against visible and invisible enemies so that we may be freed from their impediment and may lead our lives according to your divine commandments. Through Christ, our Lord. Amen.

2. SECOND DAY: Antiphon of Saint Gabriel Nuncio.

The Angel came unto Mary and said: Hail, full of Grace, the Lord is with thee; blessed are thou among women.

V. The Angel of the Lord announced to Mary. Alleluia.

R. And she conceived of the Holy Spirit. Alleluia.

Let us pray. Prayer.

O God who loves human health, to you who sent Gabriel Prince assistant and minister of your strength to proclaim to the glorious Immaculate Virgin the sacrament of the Incarnation of your Son, our Lord Jesus Christ, we humbly petition and ask that we may come under the protection of such a great Paranymph and through his intercession, you may grant us strength against the visible and invisible enemies. Through Christ, our Lord. Amen.

3. THIRD DAY: Antiphon of Saint Raphael Physician

Prince Raphael said: I am one of the Seven who stand before the Lord. And he enlightened the blind Tobit, captured the demon and relegated him to the desert.

V. Peace be with you, do not be afraid. Alleluia.

R. The Lord has fulfilled your prayers. Alleluia.

Let us pray. Prayer.

O God, who through your ineffable goodness ordained the blessed Raphael as a companion for your faithful pilgrims, and from the beginning you made him a Medic of the sick; we pray that you open the way of salvation for us who ask for the help of the aforesaid assistant Prince, and grant us healing medicine for the sickness, both of the soul and of the body. Through Christ, our Lord. Amen.

4. FORTH DAY: Antiphon of Saint Uriel Strong Companion.

O Uriel, splendor of the Divine Majesty and strength of the undefeated power, flame of ablaze charity, illuminate our minds so that we are not induced into temptation and preserve us with the sword of your power.

V. Extend, we ask, your sword, O Holy Uriel.

R. In aid of your devotees.

Let us pray. Prayer.

O God, for your incomparable mercy you associated with us your faithful Blessed Uriel, minister of the ineffable charity of your illumination, as an ardent Strong Companion who chases away the temptations of the devil; we pray that we, who resort to the defense of so much splendor, may cast out the darkness from our mind, may come to know those things that are healthy for us, and that in everything we may escape the secret pitfalls of the devil. Through Christ, our Lord. Amen.

5. FIFTH DAY: Antiphon of Saint Sealtiel Orator.

Great minister solicitor of God's mercy and noble advocate of all the faithful, we pray that you, blessed Sealtiel, consider our human frailty; so that you do not abhor our grave excesses and thus not disdain to always pray for us and you imitate our Redeemer Jesus, who seated at the right hand of the Father, the Eternal God, deigns to be our advocate.

V. Let us invoke the help of Blessed Sealtiel.

R. So that we merit forgiveness.

Let us pray. Prayer.

O God, inexhaustible source of mercy, from the beginning You wanted blessed Sealtiel to be the suppliant minister of your mercy for the sins of our human frailty; humbly we ask you that through the patronage of such a patron and for the prayer of such an Orator, you deign to free us from all impending evil and to cancel our iniquities according to the multitude of your mercies. Through Christ, our Lord. Amen.

6. SIXTH DAY: Antiphon of Saint Jehudiel Remunerator.

O Jehudiel, watchful spectator of our works and likewise remunerator, Minister of the wisdom of God, guardian of Virgins, who gives the crown to those who combat legitimately, and who punishes with the scourge those who have erred: give us counsel and help, again we pray that you speedily rise us from offending errors.

V. O Lord, prevent us with your mercy.

R. Before we feel the scourge of your anger because of our sins.

Let us pray. Prayer.

O God Almighty and just estimator of all actions, humbly we pray that through Saint Jehudiel, minister of your good advice and by you made the Remunerator, who in truth gives the rewards to the good and inflicts punishment on the reprobate: that you send to us who implore the name of a prince of such good counsel and just rewards, your illuminating grace to direct our acts in your law, and you cancel the scourge that you may have send us for our sins. Through Christ, our Lord. Amen.

7. SATURDAY: Antiphon of Saint Barachiel Auxiliary.

O Saint Barachiel, minister of the gifts of the Holy Spirit and minister of divine grace and blessing, pray to God that He may instill in us the spirit of fortitude, the spirit of wisdom, the spirit of truth, with which we can resist the snares of demons, the fragility of the body and the world, as well as resist darkness and sin, and that we may do holy work.

V. Give us, Lord, the gifts of the Holy Spirit.

R. For the intercession of Saint Barachiel who assists before you.

Let us pray. Prayer.

O God, dispenser of all that is good, grant us, we pray, your help and grace without which we can do nothing, so that by the inspiration of the Holy Spirit, we who apply ourselves to good works, merit to have Saint Barachiel Auxiliary to remove the doubts of our minds, so that we may know those things that are harmful to us, and so that once our senses are reassured we may become vessels for your blessings and your eternal grace. Through Christ, our Lord. Amen.

APPENDIX

SACRED IMAGES
HALOS AND EMBLEMS
PLATES

The images in this booklet were already considered "antique" 500 years ago. Their antiquity was precious to Antonio del Duca in the 16th century and it should be to us now. The 2nd-5th century frescoes found in the church of Palermo confirmed the identity of the Seven Angels in a time-tested manner, meaning that these seven entities had been contacted by name for centuries with good results. It may well be that the antiquity of the images is even more precious today when so many New Age Angels' invocations and images are being "channeled" and presented to the public without genuine proof that the spirits being contacted are bona fide holy Spirits of God.

Sacred images, icons and illustrations, are tools to in-spire, that is, to fill the viewer with spirit. The antique illustrations in this booklet are like celestial portals that open the communication with those spirits that reside in Heaven. To imagine the particular appearance of each individual Angel facilitates the perception of his presence.

Suggested Exercise for the Visualization of the Angels Presence

Generate in your heart sincere gratitude and thank God for having placed these heavenly spirits of great sanctity and dignity at the service of man.

Familiarize yourself with each Angel's iconographic elements, the meaning of his name, his title, his motto, his number and the symbolism of his personal implements.

Then recite or chant the Angel antiphon and prayer. It is said that this recitation should be heartfelt and not mechanical. Love for the Angels naturally blossoms when we get to know them. At first the feeling of positive emotion may be generated from the wish to thank God for the creation of His Holy Angels or from the desire to honor the Princes or from the certainty that God will send them to our aid.

Make your breath easy and even. Smile, relax your gaze and rest your eyes softly and without strain on the Angel's image. After a moment of contemplation, close your eyes. As your breath gently goes in and out, visualize a warm, pure, brilliant light descending from Heaven. Imagine that from this bright light emerges an Angel. Envision the radiant Angel with his implements.

The Septenary is a devotion that is practiced over seven consecutive days. The Seven Princes Septenary starts on a Sunday, on the day that Archangel Michael is honored; Gabriel is honored on Monday; Raphael on Tuesday; Uriel on Wednesday; Sealtiel on Thursday; Jehudiel on Friday and on Saturday, Barachiel. Light a white candle, recite each day the opening prayers and then add the particular antiphon and prayer for the Prince of the day.

It is said that if what we requested is granted, we should express gratitude to the Lord and to His Seven Princes for the favor. Many devotees offer alms-giving in the Princes' names, for instance seven new pieces of clothing for seven needy people, or a small food donation to seven food banks.

What day of the week was your date of birth? It is a folk custom to pay extra attention to the Prince that corresponds to the day of the week when the person was born. If you don't know it, you may find out by searching Google. If you were born on a Saturday your number is 7 and your Prince is Barachiel, the Angel Blessings of God and every Saturday should be special for you.

The symbol called the *Globus Cruciger*, the cross-bearing orb, appears in several illustrations. In Ancient times the orb symbolized authority, may it be the authority of a god like Jupiter or of an emperor. Around the 5th century the cross was added to the orb to represent Christ dominium.

HALOS

A *halo* or *nimbus of sanctity* is a symbolic circle of light that surrounds the head of a figure to indicate a holy person. It represents the light of divine grace permeating the soul and the body. A *cruciform halo* is used to represent Jesus or the persons of the Holy Trinity. The equilateral *triangular halo* is often used on its own as a simple way to represent the Trinity or shown on the person of God the Father. The *starry halo* also called the circle of twelve stars is shown only on the Virgin Mary and it is a reference to the Woman of the Apocalypse, Revelations 12:1. A radiant halo emanating from the whole body is called an *aureole of glory*; the aureole of glory is commonly use for the Trinity or for each of the Persons if they are portrayed on their own; it is also seen around Mary, most commonly when she is shown pregnant or with the Divine Child on her lap. A *mandorla,* meaning almond nut, is a aureola formed by the intersection of two disks; there are no mandorlas in Duca's booklet. The *Sunburst emblem* seen in the monograms of Jesus and Mary is a solar symbol of ancient origin. Even if the Angels are pure energy and radiate light through their whole being, they are normally portrayed only with a *halo of sanctity.*

EMBLEMS

An emblem is a symbolic artifact that represents concepts using pictorial images.

The Emblem of the Holy Name of Jesus

The emblem of the Holy Name of Jesus originated in Rome with the early Christians. The monogram IHS (or YHS) consists of Latin letters corresponding to the Greek iota, eta, and sigma, the first three letters of the name IHSOUS (pronounced Iesous, Greek for Jesus).

A back-formed acronym, that is a later interpretation of the three letters, gives them the meaning, JESUS HOMINUS SALVATOR, "Jesus Savior of Men".

In a further development, a cross is mounted on the horizontal stroke of the H. Often three nails are placed below the three letters and the cross. These nails are known as the Three Nails of Christ Cross even if it is not known how many nails were used in the crucifixion. Another secondary interpretation of this emblem derives from the observation that the nails form the letter "V" below IHS. IHSV came to be interpreted as IN HOCO SIGNO VINCES, "In this sign, you shall conquer".

The Sunburst Emblem

The Sunburst is a solar symbol of ancient origin preceding Christianity. It consists of rays radiating out from a central disk in the manner of sunbeams. Its use got St Bernardine of Siena, a Franciscan friar and preacher, in trouble. St. Bernardine popularized the devotion of the Holy Name of Jesus using the emblem of the Sunburst around the initials IHS in the 14th century. For this he stood trial in Rome on charges of heresy accused of creating a prophylactic amulet. He was found innocent and Pope Martin V requested him to preach in Rome, which he did for 80 consecutive days.

Don C. Skemer in *Binding Words: Textual amulets in the Middle Ages*, writes on page 115: *Paradoxically he [St. Bernardine] had been preaching about the efficacy of the Holy Name of Jesus as potent weapon against demons plagues and other misfortunes. When delivering his fiery sermons, he held up a square tablet on which was inscribed the sacred YHS monogram standing for "YHESUS" or "YHESUS homine salvator" encircled by a sunburst. In effect, the latter transformed the Holy name into a magical seal, which St. Bernardino urged crowds to venerate as protection against divine wrath. We know (and surely he must have known) that divine names, including YHS monogram, had long been standard fare in textual amulets. But he offered it alone, as an emblem of divine power, and not as one among the many divine names found in amuleteic texts.*

The Emblem of the Sacred Heart of Jesus

The Sacred Heart of Jesus is symbolized by a triumphant bleeding heart pierced by a lance or by three nails, and/or a crown of thorns. The devotion to the Most Sacred Heart of Jesus, *Sacratissimum Cor Iesu,* is one of the most widely practiced Roman Catholic devotions, taking the Heart of the resurrected Body as the representation of the Love of Jesus Christ God. Jesus' heart pierced on the Cross reveals God's boundless and passionate love for mankind. We don't know who the first devotees of Sacred Heart were, but indications of this devotion are found in the 11th and 12th centuries in Benedictine and Cistercian monasteries.

The Emblem of the Society of Jesus, the Christogram of the Jesuits

The Society of Jesus is a scholarly religious congregation of the Catholic Church that originated in Spain in the 16th century. In 1541 St. Ignatius of Loyola, founder of the Society of Jesus, adopted the popular emblem IHS with the cross and three nails as the insignia of the Order. Since then the emblem has become a strong indicator of the Jesuit presence. The Jesuits became the main propagators of the symbolic language of emblems and allegories because emblematic imagination is central in their educational system.

The Emblem of the Christogram does not appear in the first two editions of the booklet but it appears three times in the last two editions including on the title page. This indicates that the Naples 1594 and 1604 editions were published after Duca's death by the Jesuits. I have a feeling that these two editions were intended for Jesuit insiders and not for the public.

Eventually the old ban to print in any form the Seven Princes' names was enforced and no new editions were published. One hundred years later copies of the booklet were a highly valued resource and were passed discretely among Jesuit theologians. In 1707, during a softening of the Inquisition, Father Andres Serrano writes: *The prayers and antiphonies along with the old images of these seven Angels were printed in Naples in 1604 in a small book which had the license to print from the Superiors that I took out of our Professed House of the Society of Jesus in Rome, by donation that was made to me by our Reverend Father General Miguel Angel Tamburini.*

Antonio del Duca was not a Jesuit but he found strong support for the Seven Princes in the members of the Society of Jesus as well as with the Spanish Royals and the Habsburgs. My forefather the Holy Roman Emperor Charles II became the head of the Imperial Order of the Seven Princes of the Angels.

THE PLATES

The frescoes found in 1516 under the plaster of the ancient church of Palermo were set in a triptych, that is, in three panels:

1. The Creation of the world and of the angels, with Lucifer still seated at the left hand of God and St. Michael standing in front of the throne of God.

2. The victory of St Michael over Lucifer. The Expulsion of Adam and Eve from Paradise. Abraham kneeling at the arrival of the three Angels and Abraham in the act of serving food to the Angels.

3. The Seven Princes of the Angels with their names, symbols and epithets in this position:

In the center:
Michael Victorious, in the act of crushing the dragon under his feet.

To the right side of St Michael:
Gabriel Nuncio, with a candle lit inside of a lantern and a mirror of jasper. Uriel Strong Companion, with a sword in his hand and a flame by

his feet. Raphael Doctor, in the act of guiding his protégé and holding a vial of medicine.

To the left side of St. Michael:
Sealtiel Orator, collected in pious prayer. Jehudiel Remunerator, with a crown and a whip. Barachiel Auxiliary, distributing flowers.

Only the Venice 1543 edition gives a title to each biblical vignette and arranges the vignettes in the chronological order of the Creation's events. In the later editions the order of the same vignettes was changed and they were placed in the same numerical/numerological order 1 to 7 that was attributed to the Apocalyptic Princes.

Antonio del Duca assigns one of the ancient vignettes as seen on the wall paintings to each one of the Angel Princes. He gives a title to each vignette and this title suggests one of the possible connections between the Prince and the scene depicted. In the later editions a similar goal is achieved by inserting a biblical reference within the image.

This is how del Duca titles the vignettes in 1543 and to what Angel he assigns it:

Creatio Mundi, The Creation of the world: The Gold Candlestick, the Seven Spirits, the Seven Princes of the Angels.
Creatio angelorum, The Creation of the Angels: St. Gabriel.
Rebellio Luciferi, The Rebellion of Lucifer: St. Jehudiel.
Preparatio ad bellum, The Preparation for war: St. Raphael.
Defectio luciferi , The Defection of Lucifer: St. Michael
Ade expuldio, The Expulsion of Adam: St. Uriel.
Abraam tres vide & unum adorat, Abraham saw three and adored one: St. Sealtiel.
Policentur seminis propagationem, They promise the propagation of the seeds: St. Barachiel.

TITLE PAGE

The Christogram Emblem is draped on an architectural frame reminiscent of an ancient temple. The frame features the Green Man supported by two columns sculpted in the form of a man (atlantes). The Green Man is a pagan nature spirit that became a symbol of man's dependence on nature and of the renewal of the cycles of growth. The same symbol appears in many Christian Churches across Europe, as for example in the Knights Templar's Roselyn Chapel.

PLATE page 11

This illustration appears only in the later editions.

The image is a traditional representation of the Christian Guardian Angel. Over his head the motto: *Demons I restrain.* He is shown sheltering under his left arm his protégée from the demon and with the other hand pointing to the Christogram. The banner ANGELI CUSTODIS MINISTERIA, Ministry of the Guardian Angels, wraps around IHS, the abbreviation of the Holy Name of Jesus that presides over the image. The four cartouches are titled: *Teaches and Illuminates, Inclines towards good, He defends during the agony* (time of death), *He leads to Paradise.*

Psalm 90 in the Latin Vulgate corresponds to Psalm 91 in the King James version: *For he shall give his angels charge over thee, to keep thee in all thy ways. They shall bear thee up in their hands, lest thou dash thy foot against a stone.*

This picture presents an uncommon detail: The Angel is depicted with a normal Angel halo of sanctitude but there is a trans-lucid triangle standing on his head. It emphasizes the presence of the Triune God of the Christians.

Angels have no gender yet this Guardian Angel is clearly "feminized". His arms are muscular but the lines of his chest are curved and rounded to indicate his gentleness and nurturing nature.

PLATE page 12

HAIL, QUEEN OF HEAVEN.
HAIL, MISTRESS OF THE ANGELS.

Queen of Heaven is one of the titles given to Mary by Christians of the Roman Catholic Church, the Eastern Orthodox Church and some in the Anglican Church. The title is a logical consequence of the First Council of Ephesus in the fifth century, in which Mary was recognized and proclaimed "Theotokos", in Latin, "Mater Dei" or "Deipara" and in English, "Mother of God". She, who by nature is inferior to the Angels, is in dignity superior to them, due to the fact that she has the supreme dignity of being the Mother of God. The Deipara is the Queen of Heaven and thus the Lady of the Angels.

That Mary is the Lady of the Angels is of great practical importance to us because she is set above the Angels and she is the nearest being to God, and because she is also our Mother, our advocate, our mercy, our life, our sweetness, our hope, there is no limit to the confidence we can place in her intercession.

Most of the images that portray Mary as the Queen of Heaven capture the solemn moment of her coronation by the Holy Trinity witnessed by the Angels. The moment of the coronation is a transcendental subject of contemplation but the engraving titled, *Hail, Queen of Heaven,* found in *Septem Principibus Angelorum Orationes cum ántiquis Imagibus,* Naples 1594 and 1604, paints a different scene. There is no crown and no coronation and instead it offers a glimpse of what it is about Mary that subjugates the mighty Angels. And that is the tender sight of their Sovereign Mistress as a very young maiden with her baby.

Mary is seen holding the Holy Child Jesus in her lap, indicating that she is the Throne of God. The Child's hair is golden symbolizing the connection between Jesus and the Sun. Mother and Son are shown with the halos of sanctitude. Their figures radiate an aureole of glory.

The scene is blissful. Mary is seated over the crescent of the Moon, a reminder of Revelations but she is not shown with the starry halo and there is no dragon. Multitudes of Angels enraptured in contemplative adoration surround the divine Mother and Son. She is looking to the left and far away. Her right hand covers her heart. What is she thinking? Her reflective gaze to the left may indicate that she is contemplating a scene from the past or remembering an absent loved one; the hand over the heart may indicate sorrow or concern. The divine Child has his eyes on his Mother's pensive face. In his left hand He holds the Book of the Gospels, the book that tells their life story. Perhaps Mary is remembering how much she and her Son suffered on Earth to save humankind. He rests his right hand over her hand, over her wounded heart, comforting her. But the Deipara is also our Mother and so it may be that her gaze to the left indicates that even in the Bliss of Heaven she is always thinking about us and she keeps at all times an eye on her children who cry for her intercession and help from this valley of tears.

Hail, O Queen of Heaven.
Hail, O Lady of Angels.
Hail, thou root, hail, thou gate,
From whom unto the world, a light has arisen.

Rejoice, O glorious Virgin,
Lovely beyond all others,
Farewell, most beautiful maiden,
And pray for us to Christ.

V. Allow me to praise thee, O sacred Virgin.
R. Against thy enemies give me strength.

Ave Regina Caelorum is one of four Marian antiphons. The origins of this prayer are unknown but it can be found already fully formatted in a twelfth-century manuscript. Centuries later, on January 13, 1864, Blessed Father Louis-Édouard Cestac was struck with a vision of devils scattered throughout the earth, causing unspeakable devastation. At the same time, he had a vision of the Most Blessed Virgin. Our Good Mother told him that the devils were let loose in the world and that the hour had come to pray to her as Queen of Angels, asking to send the Holy Legions to fight and put an end to the powers of Hell.

"Mother," said the priest, "thou who art so good, couldst thou not send them without being asked?"

"No," answered the Most Blessed Virgin. "Prayer is a condition set by God Himself to obtain graces."

"So Mother," replied the priest, "wouldst thou thyself teach me how one must pray to thee?"

And he received from the Most Blessed Virgin the prayer, *August Queen*:

August Queen of Heaven, sovereign mistress of the angels! Thou who from the beginning hast received from God the power and mission to crush the head of Satan, we humbly beseech thee to send thy holy legions, that, under thy command and by thy power, they may pursue the evil spirits, encounter them on every side, resist their bold attacks, and drive them hence into the abyss of woe. WHO IS LIKE GOD?

To Mary's words, Father Cestac added the closing formulae:

O good and tender mother, thou shalt always be our love and our hope. O mother of God, send thy holy angels to defend us and drive far from us the cruel enemy. Holy Angels and Archangels, defend us and keep us.

Note that in Hebrew, Who is like God? is said, *MICHAEL.*

Pope St. Pius X on 8 July 1908 declared 300 days of indulgence each time August Queen is recited. An indulgence is a means to purify the soul from the negative karma that one may have accumulated during life on this earth.

PLATE page 14

The image portraits the Christian Celestial Hierarchy. This elaborate plate is not included in the earlier 1543 and 1555 editions. The symbolic details are extraordinary considering their size. Under it reads: *Where were you when the morning stars sang together, and all the sons of God shouted for joy?* Job 38

On the top and center an aureole of glory parts the clouds to show the Triune God. The Three Divine Persons are enthroned and guarded by a winged Tetramorph, the Four Living Creatures, the bull, the eagle, the lion and the man-Cherub. The Tetramorph appears in the vision of Ezequiel and later in the Book of Revelation. It was adapted by early Christians to represent the four Evangelists.

The Father and the Son's index fingertips touch merging with the light of the Holy Spirit who is depicted as a descending dove. The dove is an emblem of purity, benignity and peace; the Holy Spirit came down in the form of a dove on the occasion of the baptism of Jesus in the Jordan and in Gen. 8:11, the dove carried the olive branch of peace after the flood. The Father, shown as an elder with a triangular equilateral halo, holds in his left hand an open book, the symbol that all things are open to the omniscient eye of God. The Son sits at the right hand of the Father and holds in his right hand a scepter or a rod, symbolizing his Kingship.

From the Oneness of the Three Persons appears what could be a bright orb of light or it could be what is mysteriously described in Revelation 4:6: *Before the throne there was as it were a sea of glass, like crystal.* From it, the creative power like a mighty river of divine life-giving waters flows down through the spirits' spheres until it manifests the physical realm.

On the left side of the image but a little bit lower, the heavenly clouds open to show Mary, Mother of Jesus. She is turned to face the Holy Trinity and she is seated in blissful contemplation. Her hands join over her rounded womb that emerges luminously between the darker shades of her robe like a new Sun. A bright and radiant aureole of glory emanates from her pregnant body. Her head is surrounded by a halo of twelve stars reminiscent of Revelations.

Immediately under these presiding enthroned figures stand Seven Angels. Each of these Standing Seven is portrait as an individual and this is indicated by the different implements that each one holds. On the left side the Angel holding the Standard of the Cross and a victory palm branch is Michael, the leader of the Angelic Armies. Next to him the Angel with a sword in his right hand and a flame by his feet is Uriel and Raphael is the one holding the hand of his human protégé young Tobias and a vial of medicine. On the other side we see Gabriel holding a mirror and a light inside of a lantern; Jehudiel, holding a crown and a whip; Sealtiel holding his hands in the gesture of humble prayer and finally Barachiel holding the fragrant flowers of the God's Heavenly Garden in his robe. The seven Angels are portrayed with halos.

Below the Seven that stand in the presence of God, the Nine Choirs of Angels are depicted kneeling and positioned in triads on three levels or Spheres. These Angels are not presented as individuals but as uniformed multitudes. All the Angels belonging to the same Choir hold the same implement. The absence of halos is surely a design strategy to keep clean lines in the miniature representation of the angelic multitudes.

First Sphere, the Angels ministering directly to God:

1. The first Choir, the Seraphim. These Angels burn with divine love and so they are shown presenting their hearts to God. They are said to constantly sing God's praises: *Holy, holy, holy is the Lord of Hosts.* The Seraphim have six wings, two cover their faces, two cover their feet and two are for flying. Because the image is so small, it may seem that the Seraphim are shown with only four wings set on their back, two emerging from their shoulders pointing down and two behind their head pointing

up; but the third pair of wings is present, look closely at what at first glance seems to be their legs and you will notice that they are wings.
2. The second Choir, the Cherubim. They are the guardians of God's glory and symbolize God's power and mobility. These Angels are the embodiment of the wisdom of God and they are positioned directly under the Tetramorph thus signifying that they are of the same nature as this unearthly creature, even if here they are depicted with one face instead of four. The divine Wisdom is symbolized by the open book they hold.
3. The third Choir, the Thrones. These Angels are living symbols of God's throne of justice and authority but these are Angels of pure humility, submission and peace. They reside in the zone where material form begins to take shape. They only grant passage to the spirits of God and the souls of the righteous; even the lower Angels have to pass by them to access God.

Second Sphere, the Angels ministering directly to Nature (the created Universe):

4. The forth Choir, the Dominions or Dominations. These are Angels of leadership. They make known God's commands and regulate the duties of the lower Angels. This is symbolized by the crown and a special scepter that is topped by an orb of light.
5. The fifth Choir, the Virtues. These Angels are perfectly connected with the Source of Virtue and Virtue flows through them abundantly to those who are positioned below in the order of Creation, filling them with virtue. Their duty is to supervise the heavenly bodies and maintain cosmic order; they control the elements and all nature is subject to their command. This is symbolized by the Globus Cruciger, the orb and the cross.
6. The sixth Choir, the Powers. These Angels wearing full armor and helmets are ready to enforce the order of the cosmos. They fight the evil spirits that create chaos in the Universe through human beings.

Third Sphere, the Angels ministering directly to Humankind:

7. The seventh Choir, the Principalities. These Angels guide and protect nations and institutions. Their duty is to carry out the orders given to them by the Dominions and bring blessings to the material world. They wear a crown on their head and they hold another crown in their hands for the princes that rule the many nations on earth.
8. The eight Choir, the Archangels. These Chief Angels are portrayed in the act of presenting scales to a central figure, their leader Michael, who is in charge of weighting the soul's deeds.
9. The ninth Choir, the Angels. The Angels of the lower Choir are closest to human beings and the physical world. They deliver prayers to God and bring God's messages to humans. They are depicted guarding the soul and carrying it to Heaven.

The bottom of the image pictures the earth realm. The Divine Spirit is like a waterfall that brings to life the garden and the city. The streets proclaim Alleluia! Praise the Lord!

PLATE page 16

This illustration from the 1594 edition depicts the sacredness of the number seven. On the left side of the image we see the Jewish Gold Candlestick of Seven arms with seven flames; under it is the notation Exod. 25. On the right side, the Creator is shown with a stylus in his right hand in the act of drawing an astrological representation of the heavens and the planets. With his left hand He is commanding the Primordial Elements to form the world. Under it is the notation Gen. 1.

In the outer circle stand the constellations. The seven visible planets are placed in concentric orbits and at the center we see the four great elements. This indicates that God created the world within the order of the other planets and that their influence (Latin *in*, into and *fluere*, to flow) pertains to the Divine Design.

The depiction of the Elements is absent from the early editions. The other three differences of how this illustration appears in the editions before and after Duca's death are:

1. The titles assigned by Duca to each vignette were not included in the later editions. In 1543 this image is titled *Creatio Mundi,* The Creation of the World.

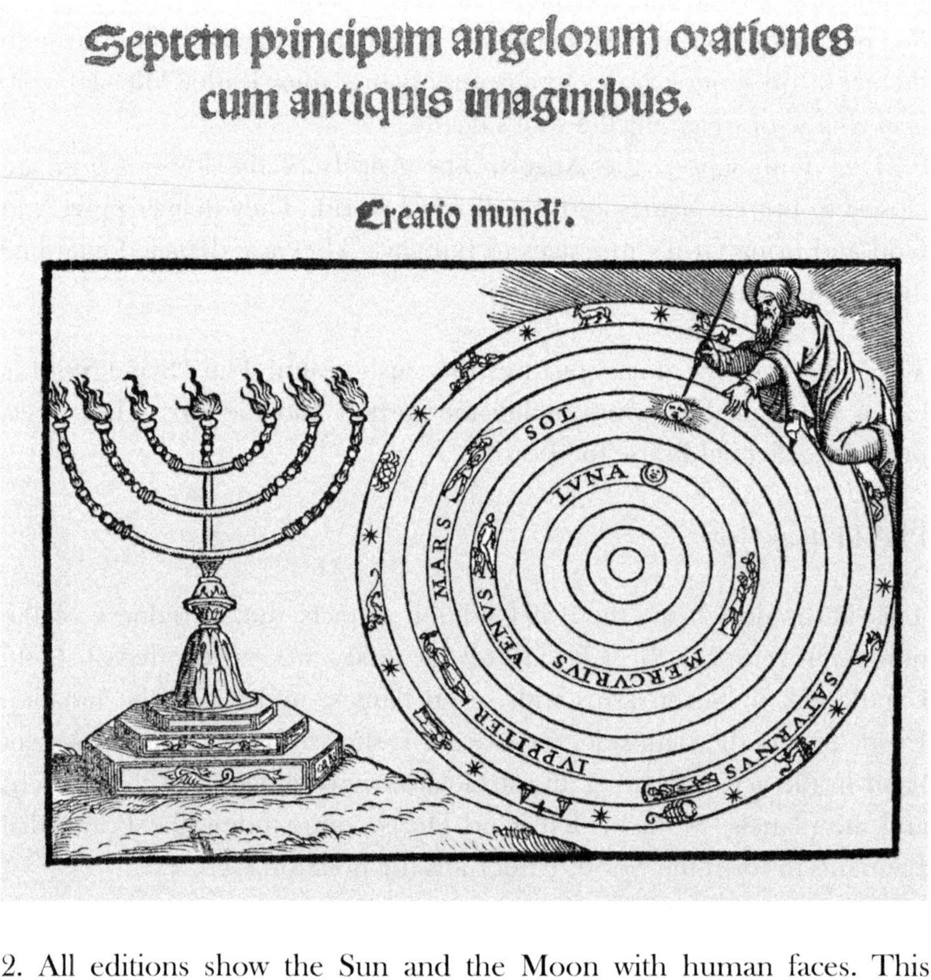

2. All editions show the Sun and the Moon with human faces. This could be interpreted as an indication that the Sun and the Moon have a "spirit". It was culturally acceptable to depict the Son and the Moon with faces as it was viewed as an old decorative device and not necessarily a spiritual statement. Also, it would not have been spiritually offensive

because since early Christianity Jesus had been associated with the Sun and His Mother Mary with the Moon in reference to the Revelations of John.

I think that it is relevant that the five tiny anthropomorphic figures of the planetary spirits that are present in Duca's illustration are not present in the later Jesuits' engraving. These five distinctive images that portray the planetary spirits as persons (imagos) are replaced in the edition of 1594 and 1606 with five identical and impersonal stars. One may think that this is an oversight or an artistic choice of the anonymous engraver that created the new plates. It was surely a strategic move dictated by the patron who commissioned the work to distance the Seven Princes of the Angels from the ancient Mediterranean seven planetary spirits traditions, which was a huge controversial subject and thereby avoided the condemnation and censure of the Inquisition.

3. The constellation Pisces is out of view in Duca's edition. The constellation Aquarius is out of view in the Jesuit edition.

PLATE page 18

This plate is a close up of the Seven Angels who stand before God. They are shown with their personal implements as we have already seen them in the Celestial Hierarchy's illustration on page 14. Their names are included in this larger format. The references are Tob. 12, Apoc. 1, Apoc. 4 and Apoc. 5. Note the young man with a fish, a reference to Raphael and the Book of Tobit.

Above the Angels and presiding over the scene stand the *Sunburst emblems of Jesus and Mary* illuminated by the light rays of the Most High. This is a symbolic simplification of the figures that previously appeared presiding over the Angels on page 14.

To the right of God's Light stands the insignia of the Sacred Name of Jesus. A new detail appears and here the three nails are shown piercing a heart, one of the symbols of the Sacred Heart of Jesus. The same

Sunburst combining the Sacred Name with the Sacred Heart emblems appears also in a Jesuit print from 1586.

To the left side is the monogram of Mary, MRA, detailed with the crown of Heaven and with a heart pierced by the sword of sorrow. The symbol of the sword originates in Simeon's prophecy in the Gospels Luke 2:35.

The *Alliance of the Hearts of Jesus and Mary* is based on the historical, theological, and spiritual links between the Sacred Heart of Jesus and the Immaculate Heart of His Mother. The Hearts of Jesus and Mary are mentioned in the New Testament. Luke 2:19 states: *Mary kept all these things pondering them in her heart,* and Luke 2:51: *His Mother kept all these things carefully in Her Heart.* John 7:38 refers to the heart of Jesus: *From His Heart will flow rivers of living water.*

The *Alliance of the Hearts of Jesus and Mary* devotion was finally formalized in the 17th century by Saint John Eudes who organized the scriptural, theological, and liturgical sources and obtained the approbation of the Church. He said: *You must never separate what God has so perfectly united. So closely are Jesus and Mary bound up with each other that whoever beholds Jesus sees Mary; whoever loves Jesus, loves Mary; whoever has devotion to Jesus, has devotion to Mary.* In the 20th century, in the reported messages of Our Lady of Fatima, it was stated that the Sacred Heart of Jesus wishes to be honored together with the Immaculate Heart of Mary.

According to Matthew 5:8*: Blessed are the pure in heart, for they will see God.* The "immaculate heart" is a heart which, with God's grace, has come to perfect interior unity with God and which constantly says yes to God and asks that His will be done; this is why we refer to Mary's Heart as *the Immaculate Heart.*

PLATE page 20

The vignette depicts St. Michael and his Angels in battle as it is described in the *Apocalypse of St. John*, Rev. 2. *Then war broke out in heaven. Michael and his angels fought against the dragon, and the dragon and his angels fought back. But he was not strong enough, and they lost their place in heaven. The great dragon was hurled down, that ancient serpent called the devil, or Satan, who leads the whole world astray. He was hurled to the earth, and his angels with him.* On the background of the celestial battlefield we see the divine light shining from above over the throne that was left empty by the arrogant spirit, the fallen one.

On the left side of the composition we see Michael crushing the dragon under his feet while holding the standard of the Cross and the palm of victory instead of the battle sword. His epithet is MICHAEL VICTORIOUS and his motto reads: *Paratus ad animas suscipiendas. Ready to receive souls.*

PLATE page 21

In the left hand panel St. Gabriel, Strength of God, is shown with a lit candle inside of a lantern and a mirror of jasper. This symbolizes that he is the first interpreter of the divine illumination. He holds the divine source of Light protected within the lantern and he proclaims it to all, which is signified by the reflecting mirror. His epithet is GABRIEL AMBASSADOR and his motto reads: *Spiritus sanctus superueniet in te. The Holy Spirit will come upon you.*

In 1543 Duca entitles the vignette, *The Creation of the Angels.* It portrays God with his right hand raised in the gesture of communication and holding the cruciform orb in his left hand. The orb and the inscription Luke 1, indicate that when God created the Angels, He illuminated them with the wisdom of the Kingdom of Jesus Christ. This is probably why Duca assigned this vignette to Gabriel. It is thought that God gave first the most important news of all creation to His supreme Ambassador and then Gabriel illuminated all the other Angels with the news.

PLATE page 22

This plate presents St. Raphael, Medicine of God, with his protégé and a vial of medicine, his title is DOCTOR OF SALVATION and his motto reads: *Viatores comitor, infirmos medico. I accompany the travelers, I heal the sick.*

Duca titles this vignette, *The preparation for war.* Later editions added the reference, Tob. 5. Before starting the dangerous journey Raphael said to old Tobit, "*Take courage; the time is near for God to heal you; take courage.*" And later, "*I will go with him* [Tobias the son]*; so do not fear. We shall leave in good health and return to you in good health, because the way is safe.*" The vignette depicts the moment before the great celestial battle. The Angelic troops are gathered and their leader Michael can be identified by the cruciform standard. God sits on a throne made of Cherubs and is represented in the act of encouraging and invigorating His Angels.

PLATE page 23

Uriel means the Fire or the Light of God. In the left pane Uriel stands with a resting sword in his hand and a flame near his feet. The fire signifies the Charity of God and the flame burning near the Angel's feet symbolizes that Uriel is prompt and ready to inflame the hearts of those who seek God. His epithet is STRONG COMPANION and his motto reads: *Flamescat igne charitas. Inflame with Charity.*

In 1543, Duca titles this vignette *Ade expuldio,* The expulsion of Adam. He assigns to Uriel the severe role played by the Angel in Gen. 3. Since Adam's time the Angel Fire of God guards the entrance to Paradise with a raised flaming sword. But here in the standing portrait Uriel is depicted with a resting sword and a flame burning bright on the ground. Most importantly he is shown wearing two bands crossing his chest and those bands are adorned with crosses. This indicates that this is Uriel after the Redemption took place and he is now ready to ignite in us the fiery desire for God so that we may find our way back to Him.

PLATE page 24

On the left side panel is a portrait of St. Sealtiel, Prayer of God, in perfect pious prayer, his hands raised to his chest in devout supplication; his head is bowed with respect and his eyes are raised humbly to the Lord. His epithet is ORATOR and his motto reads: *Oro supplex et acclinis. I pray, I supplicate and I incline.*

In 1543, Duca titles this vignette, *Abraam tres vide & unum adorat,* Abraham saw three and adored one. Later editions substitute the title by the biblical reference Gen. 18: *Then the Lord appeared to him near the great trees of Mamre, as he was sitting in the tent door in the heat of the day. So he lifted his eyes and looked, and behold, three men were standing by him; and when he saw them, he ran from the tent door to meet them, and bowed himself to the ground and said, "My Lord, if I have now found favor in Your sight, do not pass on by Your servant. Please let a little water be brought, and wash your feet, and rest yourselves under the tree. And I will bring a morsel of bread, that you may refresh your hearts. After that you may pass by, inasmuch as you have come to your servant."*

Just by looking at the picture one may think that Abraham is kneeling in front of the Angels and worshiping them but this is not the case. The three strangers are interpreted as the symbol of the mystery of the Triune and One God visiting man. In the physical realm the presence of the One was manifested by three with one voice. Duca reinforces this interpretation in the title given in the Naples edition, 1543. The vignette does not indicate that Angel Sealtiel is one of the three Angels but that Abraham and Sealtiel mirror each other in their attitude of perfect pious prayer in the presence of God: *I pray, I supplicate and I incline.* Some mystic traditions think that in this biblical moment the presence of the Triune God may also have manifested the presence of the Angels Triad of Michael, Gabriel and Raphael.

PLATE page 25

Jehudiel means *Praise of God.* His epithet is REMUNERATOR and his motto is *Deum laudantibus praemia retribuo, I reward with gifts those who praise God.* His symbolic implements are the crown and the whip.

It is important to note that in the early editions the vignette assigned to Jehudiel is different from the vignette in the later editions. The composition is very similar but the cosmic moment and the players have changed.

Venice 1543 and Rome 1555, under the title *Rebellio Luciferi* we see Angel Jehudiel standing in the left side panel. The companion biblical vignette shows the moment of Lucifer's rebellion. God is seated in a throne of light surrounded by Seraphs. God holds the implements of supreme authority, the scepter and the cross-bearing orb. His face is turn towards Lucifer with a sad expression. Lucifer is portrayed as a beautiful being with four wings indicating that he belongs to the higher Angels hierarchy but the halo of sanctitude is missing already. He is facing straight forward with arrogance, no other figure in the remaining illustrations faces forwards. Lucifer sits on a throne situated to the left hand of God, a privileged position that he occupied because he was God's favorite counselor. The two thrones are at the same level indicating the high position God placed him on or that he is challenging God's authority. The figure of Lucifer is smaller than the figure of God and he is not holding the implements of power. His right hand points down to his crotch. He is surrounded by the Angels who he has seduced and they are portrait kneeling before him with their hands in the gesture of adoration.

In the Naples 1594 and 1606 editions, the title over the illustration is omitted, instead we see the reference to Exod. 23. Jehudiel's companion vignette changes dramatically while maintaining a similar composition. Now Jehudiel sits in the left hand throne where before sat proud Lucifer, but now this throne is lower that God's. Jehudiel is portrayed with the halo of sanctitude and with four wings indicating his high status among the Angels. Around him the Angels are shown standing instead of kneeling; their hands are in the gesture of respect and not of the adoration that the seduced Angels showed before Lucifer when he sat on the same throne. Jehudiel holds the implements of Divine Justice, the crown and the whip, the punishment and the reward. It is because of the rebellion of Lucifer that punishment and reward had to sit in the vacant throne position on the left side of God's Throne. In contrast with the arrogant frontal gaze of vane Lucifer, Jehudiel's head is slightly bowed and he keeps his inner sight on his Lord. The eyes of the Lord are on Jehudiel and He is pleased.

PLATE page 26

Barachiel means the Blessing of God. His epithet is AUXILIARY and his motto: *In oportunitatis, in tribulationes ne derelinquas nos. In opportunity or in tribulation, do not abandon us.* The 1543 plate is titled is *Policentur seminis propagationem,* They promise the propagation of the seeds. Later editions show the reference Gen. 18.

The blessings of God are like fragrant flowers from His heavenly garden and so Barachiel is depicted distributing flowers. The vignette depicts Abraham's three visitors. The three figures are identical and their gestures synchronized, the one hand touching the table where the bread is set and the other raised in the gesture of benediction. Barachiel is not one of the three Angels. He is the blessing itself.

Printed in Great Britain
by Amazon

23612342R00030